For what age group is this book?

There is something for everyone to learn from this book.

This book is primarily for parents and teachers to help them educate children of all age groups about respect. It is written in a simple language so that adults can discuss this complicated subject with young children. Parents and teachers have the freedom to be innovative and they can tailor their approach according to the age of the children.

Reading this book is not sufficient; helping children to apply these thoughts in their day-to-day lives is important.

I RESPECT YOU!

Neeti Kohli, M.D.

Read this book slowly and meditate upon the thoughts!

Chapter 1 is about the basic principles of respect.

Chapter 2 is about respecting ourselves and handling our mistakes and weaknesses.

Chapter 3 is about handling mistakes of other people.

Chapter 4 is about respecting parents and teachers.

Chapters 5 & 6 are about losing and regaining respect in society.

Reinforce the message by doing various activities with children and using other resources.

Awareness Books for Children
P.O. Box 2495
Edmond, Oklahoma 73083-2495

Website: awarenessbooksforchildren.org

My special thanks to:

My husband Vivek and
my children Uday & Supriya

Randy Anderson

Ralonda Wood

Kristi Kenney

Wayne Stein

Jeannine E. Bettis

Family & Friends

This book is dedicated to Vivek, my husband, who has always focused on my positive aspects. He has brought the best out of me and has helped me understand the true meaning of respect. Quoting him, "We have to cover each other's weaknesses and boost each other's positive aspects, so that together we emerge as someone strong."

A note to all adults

I Respect You! has been inspired by the evidence-based literature from social and emotional learning. According to the Collaborative for Academic, Social, and Emotional Learning, having "relationship skills" is one of its core competencies.

Respect is a binding force that can build strong relationships. Therefore, it is very important to learn how to give and gain respect. Even though respect is subjective and the norms vary from person to person, the basic principles are the same for everyone.

The thoughts in this book originated from the Sanskrit word "Namaste." The gesture of folding hands and bowing to another person is used to greet people in some Asian cultures. Namaste means, "Keeping my ego aside, I bow to the goodness within you." In other words, whenever you greet a person, you tell them, "I respect you."

This book is for parents and teachers. It is an overview and has a lot of information. Therefore, it is best to discuss small sections at a time with the children. To start a discussion, convert the statements in this book to questions. Ask the children to give additional examples and share their stories and experiences.

Respect should be mutual. To bring about a change, it is important to discuss this subject with every child in the group.

I hope that this book can help make a difference.

Namaste and best wishes,
Neeti Kohli, M.D.

Hi! I am a Red-Heartie. I represent the goodness that is present inside every human being.

For us to be happy, it is important that we all learn to see and appreciate this goodness in each other.

We can learn this by understanding that…

We all have similarities and differences. We are alike because we have…

1. GOODNESS AND STRENGTHS
We all have kindness and affection.
We desire to help others.
We have skills and potentials.

2. NEEDS
We all need love and appreciation.
We desire to bond with others.
We all want our opinions
to be heard.

We all are different and have different opinions because we have…

Different habits, interests, talents, abilities, likes, and dislikes.

Different age, gender, looks, skin color, and health status.

Everyone has goodness, strengths, and needs.

Different religions, cultures, races, and national origins.

Different education levels, experiences, responsibilities, richness, and environment around us.

Also, we all have weaknesses, and we all make mistakes. No one is perfect. Sometimes there are misunderstandings due to poor communication. Sometimes there are rumors spread by others.

A shell made of differences, weaknesses, mistakes, misunderstandings, and rumors covers everyone's goodness, strengths, and needs.

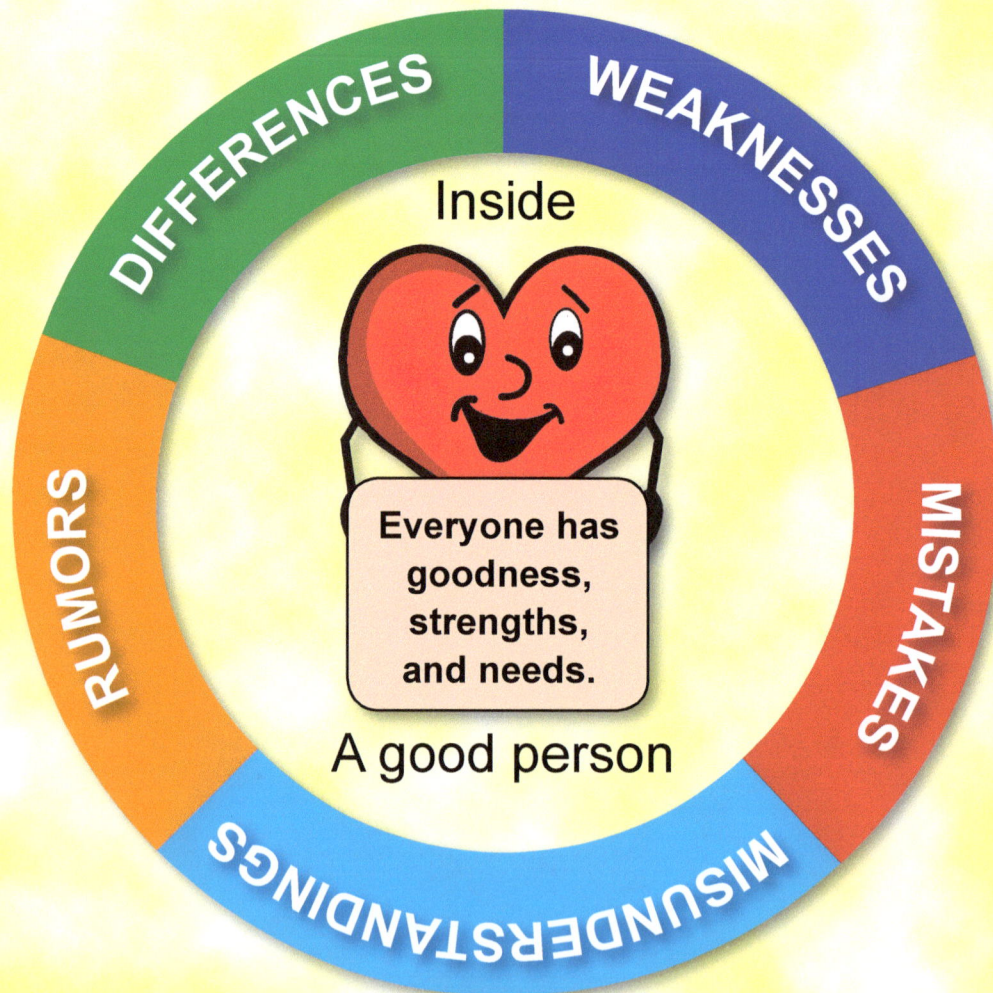

DIFFERENCES

WEAKNESSES

MISTAKES

MISUNDERSTANDINGS

RUMORS

Inside

A good person

Everyone has goodness, strengths, and needs.

When we interact with others, we can be positive or negative. We can look at the shell made of differences, weaknesses, mistakes, misunderstandings, and rumors, or we can focus on the goodness, strengths, and needs of the others.

We have to look beyond this shell to appreciate the good qualities in others and to understand their needs.

Respect is "liking people" by focusing on their positive aspects and truly appreciating their goodness and strengths. Respect is also understanding their needs and making efforts to help them selflessly.

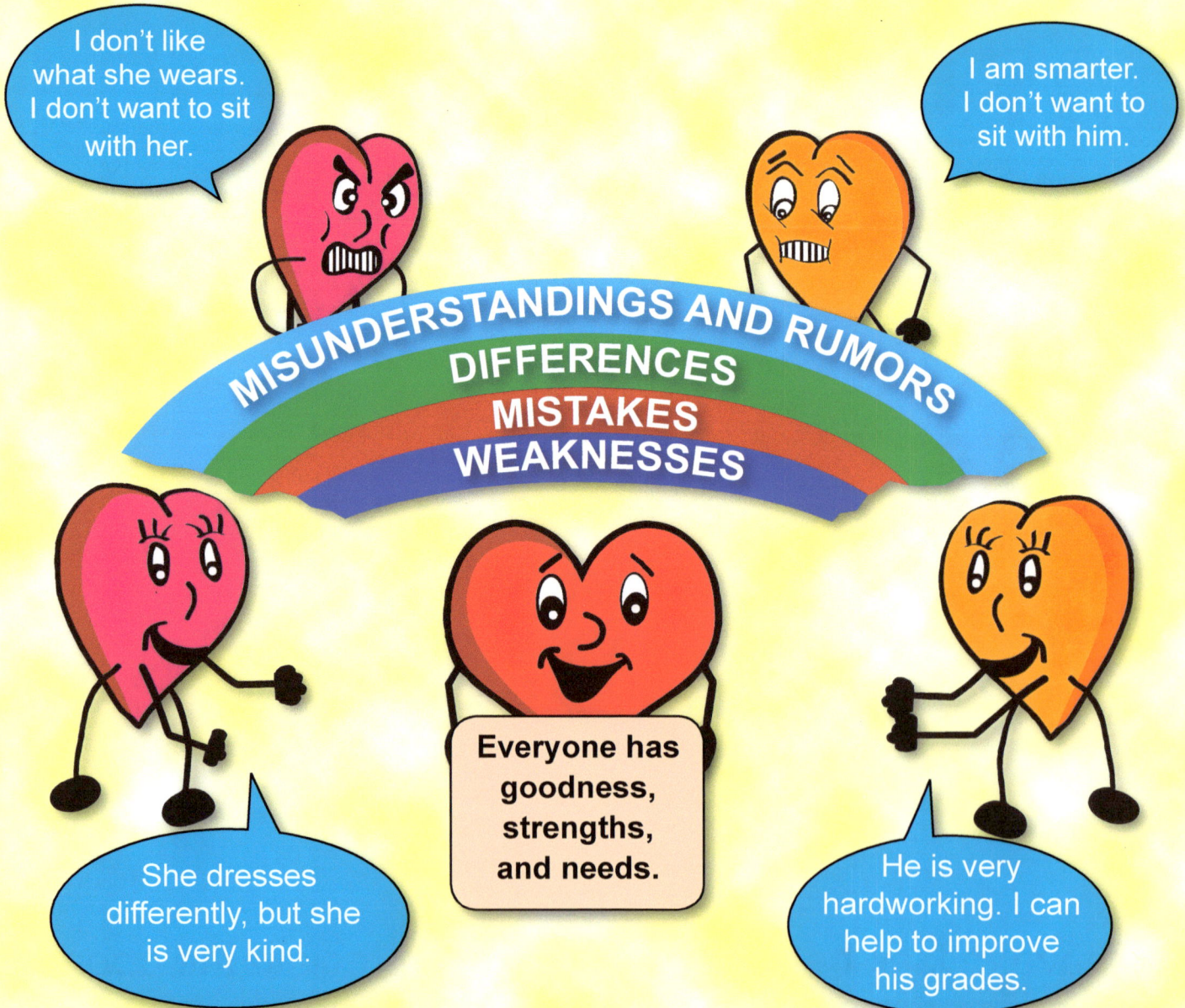

When we are able to see the goodness and strengths in others, we appreciate them. When we understand their needs, then…

We honor their wishes, and we value their time and money.

We are more willing to listen to their opinions, which may be different from ours.

We care, share, trust, and help.

We believe in equality.

I can see your goodness. I can understand your needs.

THIS IS MUTUAL RESPECT.

Respect has two components

1. Notice the good qualities of others.

Appreciate and thank.

When we truly appreciate others, we **GIVE RESPECT.**

2. Understand the needs of others.

Make selfless efforts to help.

When others truly appreciate us, we **GAIN RESPECT.**

Thank you for opening the door for me.

When we are honest, kind, and compassionate, we make it easy for others to appreciate us.

When we communicate clearly, we make it easy for others to understand our wishes and needs.

Respect is like cement!

Cement binds bricks together, builds strong buildings, and keeps the bricks united even during storms.

Respect binds people together and keeps them united even during the difficult times.

I was sick. My family and friends took good care of me.

Mutual Respect = Strong Relationships = Happiness

In a relationship, we bond with people and share our feelings. We work together as a team and progress.

However, some of our behaviors prevent us from respecting and building relationships with others. This happens when we become…

1. Egotistic and begin to put others down or want everyone to do as we wish.

2. Selfish and begin to hurt others to get more money, power, importance, or success.

You are dumb. I want you to do as I say. My way is the ONLY right way.

I want everyone to think that I am the best. I can lie and defame others to get the importance.

I want more money. I don't care if others are hurt.

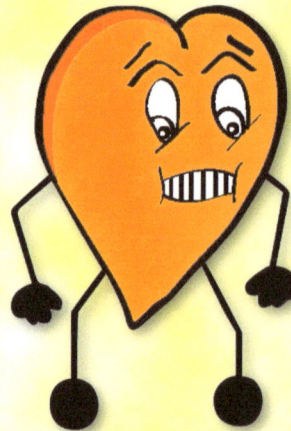

By doing so, we may get what we want, but we weaken our relationships with others. Such behaviors can bring unhappiness to our lives and to others.

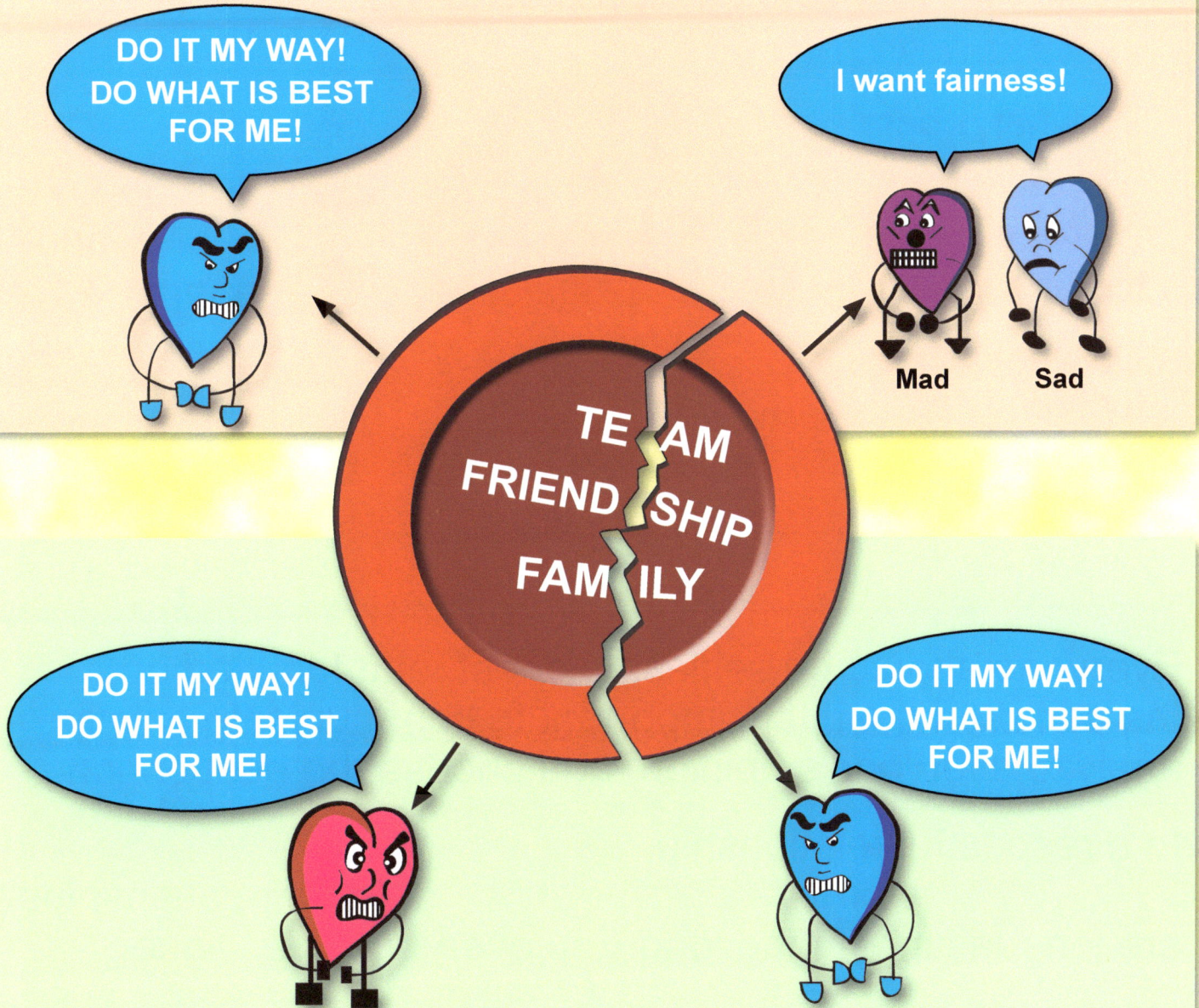

In a group, "do what is best for me" should be replaced by…

"Do what is best for the team."

"Do what is best for the family."

"Do what is best for friendship."

TEAM
FRIENDSHIP
FAMILY

A strong, caring, and happy relationship.

Everyone should be selfless, honest, and focused on the common goal. It is important to communicate calmly, analyze everyone's opinion, and choose the best option.

In a respectful relationship, everyone trusts each other and tends to compromise at different times. Such relationships are long-lasting. In the long run, everyone is a winner.

When interacting with one person, we should usually honor the wishes of that person. People have the right to pursue their own interests, passions, and religious and cultural beliefs. However, we should say no to them when…

They are hurting themselves.	They are hurting someone else or not following the rules.	They are disrupting the team.
"I want to have cookies for lunch every day." "NO! That is unhealthy."	"Let's go and tease him. It will be fun." "NO! I will not support you. This is wrong."	"I want to have the lead role in the play." "No, you cannot have that role. In the audition you got a different role."

Advise or stop others from doing something wrong.

Teach others to support the decision made by the leader of the team.

Just as we honor the wishes of others, others should honor our wishes, as well. We should not be forced to do something. Therefore, saying "no" to others is not disrespectful. We just have to learn how to communicate our wishes clearly.

CHAPTER 2 - RESPECTING OURSELVES

Commonly, we all compare ourselves to others. Such thoughts may prevent us from respecting ourselves.

When we compare, we may…

Feel **envious** if we have less than others, and we may start disliking others.

Become **sad,** develop **low self-esteem**, and forget about our own potentials.

She gets really good grades, but she is weird and annoying.

He has more toys than I do, and he goes to many fun places for vacation. I feel sad because I can't go.

I am so unfortunate. I am not beautiful. I don't want to go to the party.

Such comparisons are wrong because we are comparing one characteristic of our personality to others.

Our differences make us unique. Therefore, we should look at our personality as a whole.

Different heritage, religion, habits, interests, and appearances.

Unique means the "ONLY ONE"

Different strengths.

I am a unique person. I have different qualities. I cannot be perfect in everything.

Different weaknesses.

Something unique cannot be compared to anything else.

Different experiences and awareness about different subjects.

Because we are unique, we are all precious. Therefore, we all have an invaluable position in our family or team. We can realize our importance by imagining that one family or one team is like one human body.

I am like an "arm" of a family. If I am hurt, then the entire family feels the pain.

Member One

I am like the "eyes" of a family. I have a unique role in my family.

Member Two

I am like the "heart" of a family. I am precious.

Member Three

I am like the "lungs" of a family. No other person can replace me.

Member Four

Different body parts unite together to form one human body.
Different people unite together to form one family or a team.
Every body part is precious; similarly, every person is precious.
Body parts do not compete against each other; they work together and coordinate with each other!

We all are needed in our families and teams. Therefore, we should respect ourselves and never think about hurting ourselves.

Stay healthy and safe!

We can be happy if…

IN OURSELVES
We recognize our passions, interests, and strengths. We work hard to improve our skills and habits.

IN OTHERS
We recognize and appreciate their good qualities and skills.

When we interact with people who have different strengths, then…

1. We form a stronger team because of diverse qualities.

2. We learn good habits and skills from others.

Playing guitar is my passion and singing is yours. We form a good team.

You organize your work sheets very well. I will try it the same way.

We respect ourselves when…

We take care of our emotional needs by developing honest and sincere relationships with family members and friends.

We take care of our physical needs by taking care of our health and keeping ourselves safe.

We recognize and appreciate our strengths; feel proud of our looks, religion, culture, heritage, abilities, and monetary status; work hard to improve our skills and potentials.

Being happy is respecting ourselves!

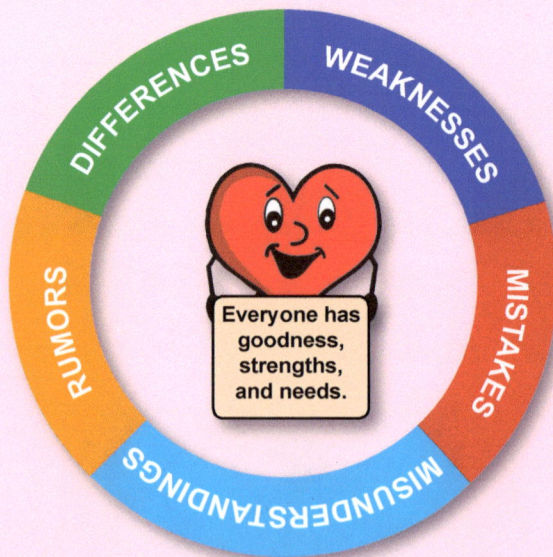

DIFFERENCES
WEAKNESSES
MISTAKES
MISUNDERSTANDINGS
RUMORS

Everyone has goodness, strengths, and needs.

No one is perfect. Having a low self-esteem is disrespecting ourselves.

Our differences, weaknesses, or simple mistakes should not make us feel envious, shameful, or guilty. We hurt ourselves by doing so.

Honest and clear communication can prevent misunderstandings and can help develop strong relationships.

We respect ourselves when we learn to…

1. Handle our weaknesses.

Form a team with a person who has a different good quality, or…

Ask for help when we are facing a difficulty or unable to solve a problem, or…

Appreciate the talents of others. Enjoy and be happy. We cannot be perfect in everything.

2. Handle our mistakes.

If we did not hurt anyone, then we should learn from our mistake and move forward.

If we hurt someone, then we should sincerely apologize and not repeat the mistake.

Apologizing for our mistakes shows a boldness of character.

We make mistakes, and others do the same. When a person makes a mistake, it is important to understand the intention.

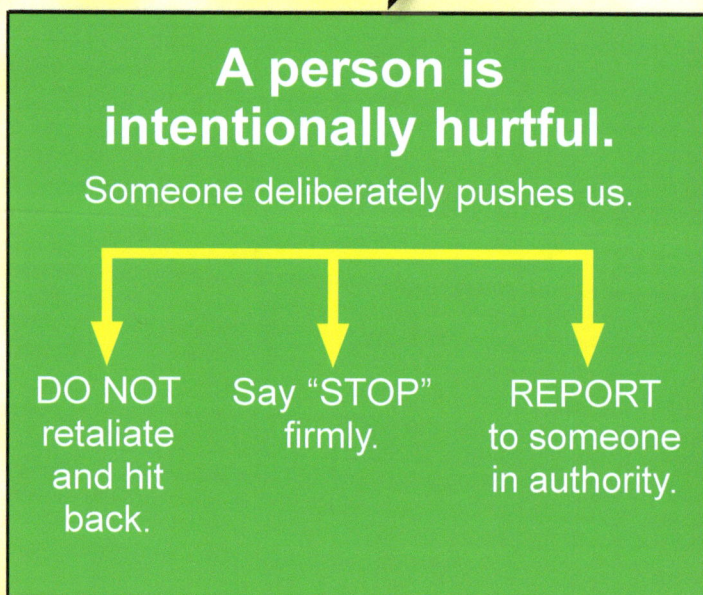

A person is intentionally hurtful.	A person is unintentionally hurtful.
Someone deliberately pushes us.	Someone trips into us by mistake.
DO NOT retaliate and hit back. Say "STOP" firmly. REPORT to someone in authority.	Accept the apology. Look beyond the mistake. Stay positive.

It is our responsibility to report to someone in authority: a parent, teacher, counselor, principal, superintendent, or law enforcement. It is the responsibility of the person who has the authority to investigate and correct the behavior, or punish the child who is hurting us.

WE SHOULD NOT HIT BACK. Instead, we should calm down. If we retaliate, then we may be punished too.

Once children who have hurt us apologize and correct their behavior, then we should look beyond their mistakes and accept them.

Accepting the apology shows strength in character.

These mentors…

HONOR OUR DIFFERENCES

IMPROVE OUR WEAKNESSES

CORRECT OUR MISTAKES

Understand our needs.

Appreciate our strengths.

Motivate, educate, and guide us to progress and be happy in life.

Their job is very difficult because they have to make us work harder, discipline us, correct our behavior, or stop us from doing something wrong. This means that they do not always let us do what we want. Therefore, we can have disagreements.

In such situations, we can either be…

Disrespectful   OR   Respectful

Criticize and speak badly about a parent or a teacher.

Keep thinking about the disagreements and forget multiple instances of helping and caring.

Communicate clearly. Understand that their actions are to help us progress.

Be appreciative and thankful.

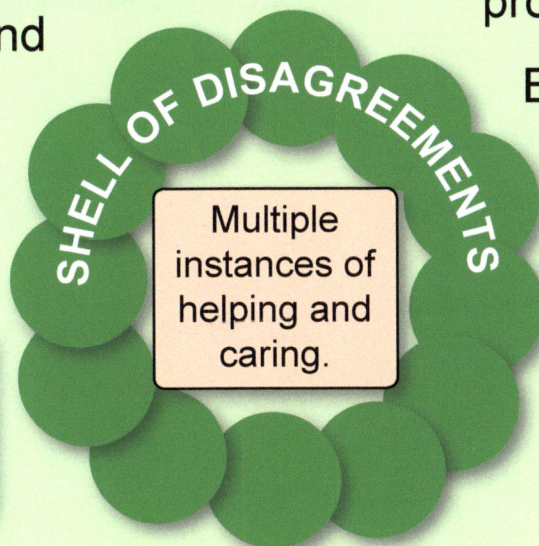

SHELL OF DISAGREEMENTS

Multiple instances of helping and caring.

"My teacher is mean. She gives me homework."

"I always do my homework and now I am really good at solving problems."

Noticing and truly appreciating the hard work, commitment, sacrifice, and dedication of our parents and teachers is respecting them.

We often disagree with people who help and care for us. Disagreements are normal, but gossiping about them is wrong because it indicates that we are disrespecting others. Also, gossiping will not resolve the disagreements. It will make the problem worse.

Sometimes, it takes time to resolve the disagreements, and we may need support. Sharing these disagreements with people whom we trust or someone who can mediate is essential.

Most parents and teachers are selfless, caring, and helpful. Unfortunately, some children do get neglected, discriminated against, or harassed. These children do not get the respect or the care that they deserve.

Therefore, it is important to report incidents of neglect, harassment, or discrimination to someone whom we trust at school or at home. If we report such things, then people in authority can help by taking a corrective action.

When we **think** badly about someone, we are focused on something that we do not like about him or her. If we **start talking** negatively about this person to our peers, then…

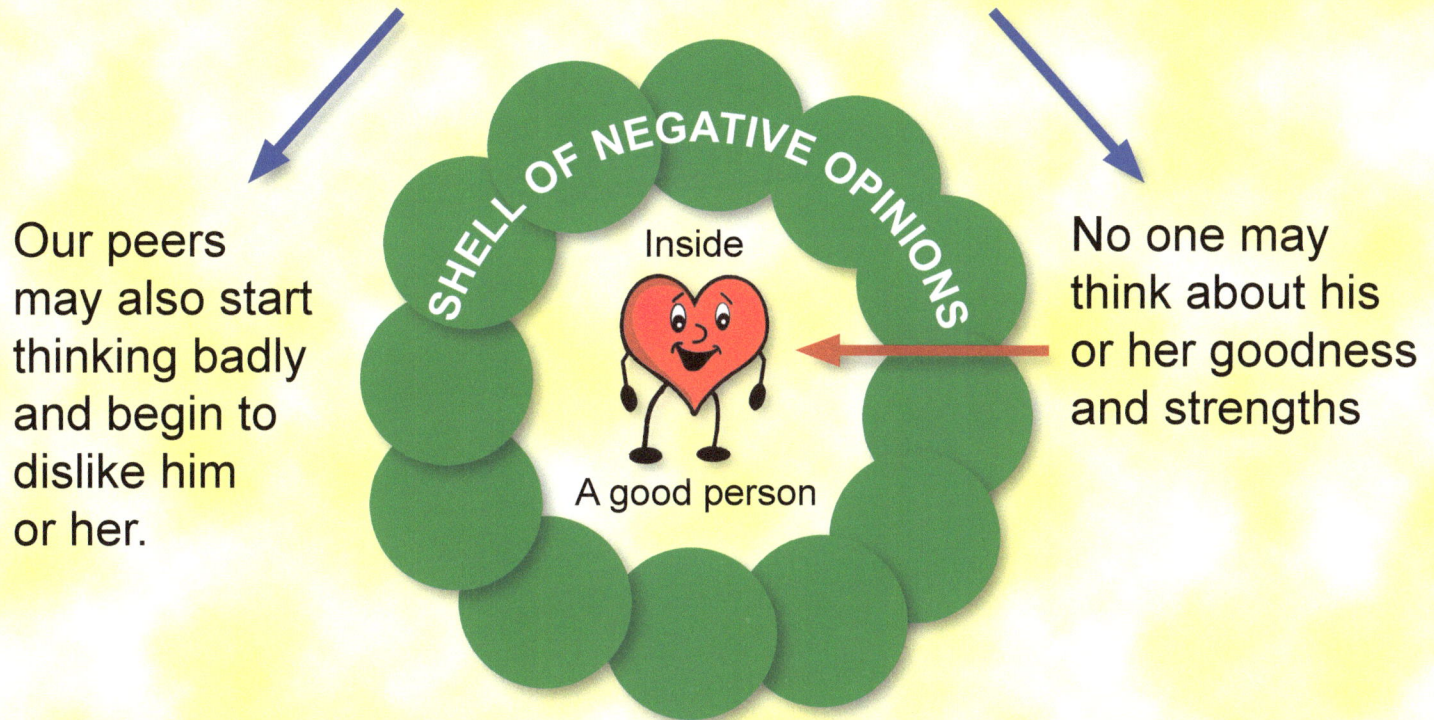

Our peers may also start thinking badly and begin to dislike him or her.

SHELL OF NEGATIVE OPINIONS

Inside

A good person

No one may think about his or her goodness and strengths

This makes someone lose respect in society because everyone is focused on something negative.

If we post our views on social media, then many people can see our opinion instantly, and it stays on the Internet permanently. Posting even one negative statement about a peer on the Internet could be considered cyberbullying. This is because that negative statement could be read again and again by other students. Then everyone will start thinking badly about that person.

The consequences of losing respect and not being liked by friends are tremendous:

Sadness

Hopelessness

Anxiety

Depression

Loneliness

Guilt

Suicidal thoughts

Shame

Poor performance

Therefore, we should not spread bad comments about anyone in person or on the Internet.

CHAPTER 6 – REGAINING RESPECT

And now, here is a story of a child who was defamed, but then she got her respect back with the help of the principal.

Nea was a kind, helpful, and caring girl. One day, someone blamed her for hurting a classmate. It was just a rumor, but everyone around her believed it to be true. No one wanted to play with her any more.

I did not hurt the other child. But no one believes me.

All she needed at that time was a kind person who could see her goodness, and understand her needs to be liked, accepted, and appreciated. This kind person was…

...the principal of the school. He investigated and found out that it was a rumor. In order to restore her respect, he appreciated her in front of the class and helped all the students to notice her goodness again. He also taught every child in the school about respect.

We should never criticize others because of their weaknesses. No one is perfect.

We should not spread bad comments about anyone by gossip or by posting on the Internet.

We should accept others as friends after they have corrected their behavior. We all make mistakes.

We are grateful for everything we have.
We are thankful to everyone who helps us.
We care, share, trust, and help others.

We are good children.
We are happy children.
Come join us!

AWARENESS CLUB FOR CHILDREN

Discuss this topic with everyone and change the environment around you!

9 781939 626103